ARYAN **TOMAR** & DR. HEECHOO

3D PRINTING AND

MAKING **DRONES** WITH **DADDY**

PROLOGUE BY **ER. VIJAI PAL**

EPILOGUE BY **ER. TOMAR V**

To order additional copies of this book, contact
Partridge India
000 800 919 0634 (Call Free)
+91 000 80091 90634 (Outside India)
www.partridgepublishing.com/india
orders.india@partridgepublishing.com

ISBN
978-1-5437-0496-9 (sc)
978-1-5437-0495-2 (e)

Print information available on the last page.

11/11/2020

PARTRIDGE

3D PRINTING AND

MAKING DRONES WITH DADDY

BY ARYAN TOMAR
& DR. HEECHOON KWON

Acknowledgment

"Dedicated to my grandparents, who molded me to who I am. To my family, who have always been there for me. To my school, who sailed through an even brighter future. And to my friends to CELEBRATE with the success. A special thanks to Dr. Kwon for mentoring me and collaborating to pull this project together. He has spent months getting to know about my life, my mind, and searched through countless workshops and memories to bring this book to life."

- Aryan Tomar

Prologue

Dear Aryan & MJ,

The idea of Making Drones with Daddy co-authored by teenager Aryan Tomar and mentored by my dear friend Dr. Drone and featuring MJ, is perfect for the young audiences. Books seem to be perfect for the millennium kids, who want to be next-gen innovators.

I cannot believe the time has gone by so fast. My teenage was a time of learning, lots, and lots of learning. They were filled with laughter and happiness but also sadness and anger. Looking back there were so many days I never thought I would make it, days I was sure I was defeated once and for all. But here I am now, hours before I enter a new decade of my life and I somehow managed to make it through it all. However, before I cheer to turning twenty, there are a few things I have to thank my teenage years for.

Thank you for all of the "firsts." This will be my first foreword for a book of Teena- ager on a topic I am so curious to explore – Drones. Your teens are a time of experiencing things for the first time and it is crazy to think of all the "firsts" I've had over the last few decades. As I look back with nostalgia on all my teenage firsts, I know my twenties will hold different, but just as many extraordinary firsts.

I have a feeling the next nine years are going to be pretty fricking awesome.

Cheers to leaving behind the days of teenage shenanigans and moving on to future careers.

Love Always,

Er. Vijai Pal

Philanthropist
Founder, Veerbala Foundation

Overview

If you hear the word 'drone,' most people's first impression is that some kind of high-tech military aircraft is flying over the clouds while the pilot is sitting in a control room hundreds of miles away.

That's not exactly what we're talking about here. More recently, the same term has been used to describe quadcopters: four-propeller remote-control aircraft. Since the flight stability and control algorithms have become more advanced, these miniature aircraft have become cheaper and more usable.

Whether you call them Unmanned Aerial Vehicles (UAVs), Miniature Pilotless Aircraft, or Flying Mini Robots, drones are becoming increasingly popular. They are still in the early stages in terms of widespread acceptance and use, but drones have already broken through rigid conventional barriers in industries that once appeared impenetrable due to similar technical advances.

In the past few years, drones have become integral to the operations of numerous companies and government agencies and have continued to pierce into areas where other sectors have either stagnated or lagged. From quick deliveries at rush hour to scanning an unreachable military base, drones are proving to be extremely beneficial in places where people are unable to perform in a timely and efficient manner.

'Making Drones with Daddy' targets the age group of teenagers and young adults who are willing to explore and learn. The book uses illustrations and explanations to attract young readers and be able to teach with infotainment.

Minjae is a drone freak, but lost when it comes to fundamentals like physics! Luckily, his father, Dr. Kwon, or Dr. Drone, a Senior Drone Specialist who uses real-world examples to help MJ and Aryan to understand the fundamentals of making a drone, and beyond! In 'Making Drones with Daddy', you'll follow alongside MJ & AT as they learn about drones and other topics like physics of everyday objects, the future of drones, the careers available, the science, terminologies, history, and much more. You will also go through the concepts of the connection between drones and virtual reality, as well as, the connection between drones and Mars.

Drones are very useful machines. In the future, knowing how to use a drone may be as useful as knowing how to read a book. The good news is that learning to build and flying drones and its fundamentals aren't as hard as learning to read. If you're mystified by the basics of a UAV or you just need a refresher, 'Making Drones with Daddy' will get you up to speed in a lively, fun, and practical way.

Authors

Aryan Tomar

a Techno-Creative Canadian teen entrepreneur, author, music producer, filmmaker, and the co-founder of TOMARS which is curating a new generation of fashion & lifestyle accessories for the Space Industry and take a leap towards sustainability. He is also a budding film director, screenwriter, and a producer. Aryan Tomar is known for being one of the youngest entrepreneurs and filmmakers.

Dr. Heechoon Kwon

an AI Professor at Caroline University, Secretary General at National Association of Cognitive Science Industries, and he is also the CEO of Mirae News and the Vice Chairman of Korean Creative Science Education Association. Dr. Kwon has achieved several awards which includes Award of Ministry Information & Telecommunication, and has also published 25+ books. He has earned his BS, MA, and Ph.D. from Sung Kyun Kwan University, his thesis was "VMME over Multimedia Framework."

Er. Vikas Tomar

spearheading Green Field venture with Korean IP. He is focused on VR Theme Parks & Immersive Infotainment IP's, in NA, S'pore & UAE. 22 years ago, he began his career as a director special effects with an Apple authorised digital studio to serve digital video services for the Hollywood industry, followed by SGI partner NetAcross as Sr. visualizer. He later served at leading new media pioneers including Rediff, NetMedia and PCCW. He holds bachelor's degree in Computer Sc. Engineering from Bangalore University and studied 3D Animation & Visual effects followed by The Producer course from VFS, Vancouver, Canada. His most recent initiatives are BTXCity (Events & Publication), and TOMARS (Space-Lifestyle Venture).

Contents

MJ is curious for Drones.

Little Minjae wants to learn about drones and what they are, but he has no idea about them, so he decides to consult his father who is a drone expert, to learn more.

01.

What is a Drone?

A quick introduction to Drones

A drone is a word that means "Buzzing." A remote-controlled unmanned aerial vehicle (UAV) that allows pilots to fly remotely without having to ride it, an UAV, commonly known as a drone, is an aircraft without a human pilot aboard. UAVs are a component of an unmanned aircraft system (UAS) which includes a UAV, a ground-based controller, and a system of communications between the two. The flight of UAVs may operate with various degrees of autonomy: either under remote control by a human operator or autonomously by onboard computers. Compared to the manned aircraft, UAVs were originally used for military missions and were defined too "dull, dirty, or dangerous" for humans. While they were originated mostly in military applications, their use was rapidly expanded to commercial, scientific, recreational, agricultural, and other applications, such as policing, peacekeeping, surveillance, product deliveries, aerial photography, agriculture, smuggling, and drone racing. Civilian UAVs have now vastly outnumbered military UAVs, with estimates of over a million sold by 2015, drones can be seen as an early commercial application in autonomous things, to be followed by the autonomous cars and home robots. The word "drone" first appeared in 1930. In 1935, the Royal Navy launched a demonstration demonstrating the use of the drone "DH82B Queen Bee." The US Navy Admiral William Standley was astonished at this maritime training. He said, "I was greatly stimulated by watching the UAV." He immediately commanded the US Navy to build

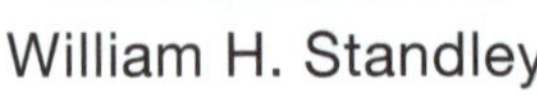

William H. Standley

DH28B Queen Bee

unmanned aerial vehicles. UAVs are now known as "Drones" everywhere globally. Drones were originally developed for military purposes, but now it's getting more and more common among people. Drones can be classified into various categories according to their purpose, structure, and function.

Structure of a Drone

The figure below is a structure of a drone including its parts and hardware.

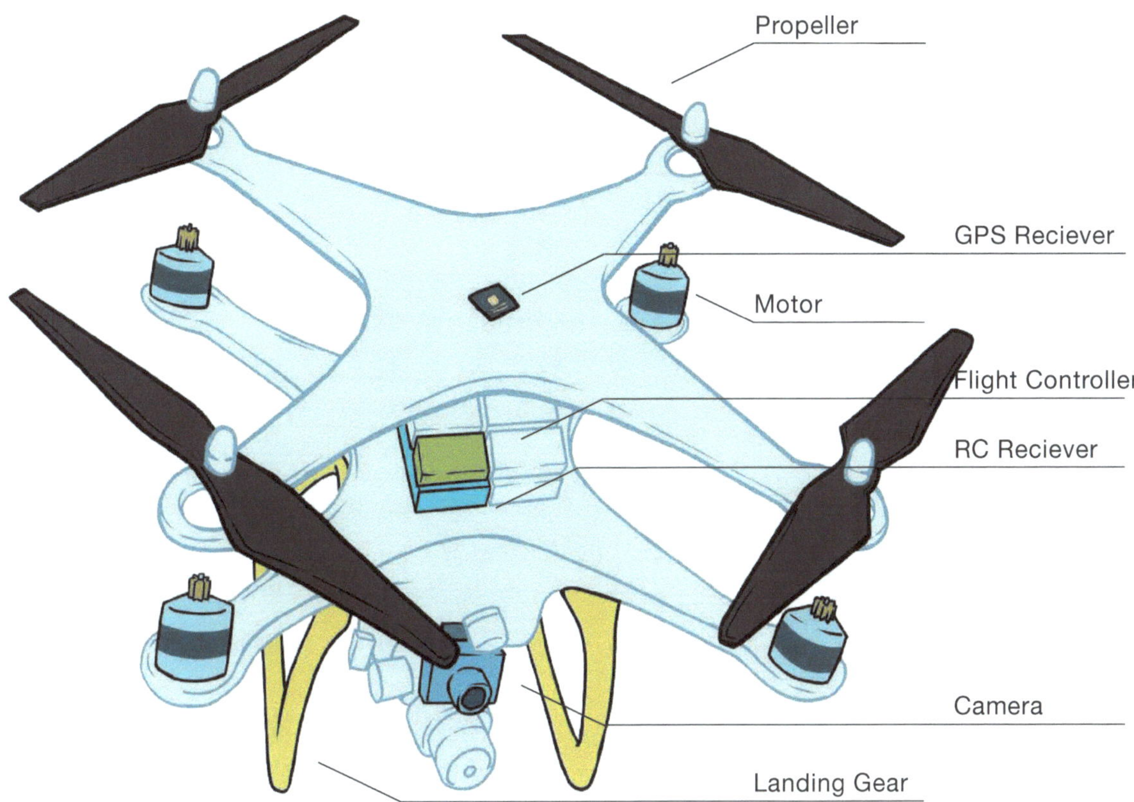

- Frame: Drone's body
- Arm: The part where the motor and propeller are mounted
- Motor: Converts electrical energy to mechanical energy
- Propeller (Rotor): Rotating blade
- Flight Controller: Automatic control of flight controlled devices (computer CPU role)
- Battery: Thinner than lithium polymer (Li-po) lithium ion and more stable with a rechargeable battery with less risk of explosion.
- Landing Gear: Protects the aircraft during takeoff and landing

Drone Controller

The figure below is a structure of a controller that controls the drone.

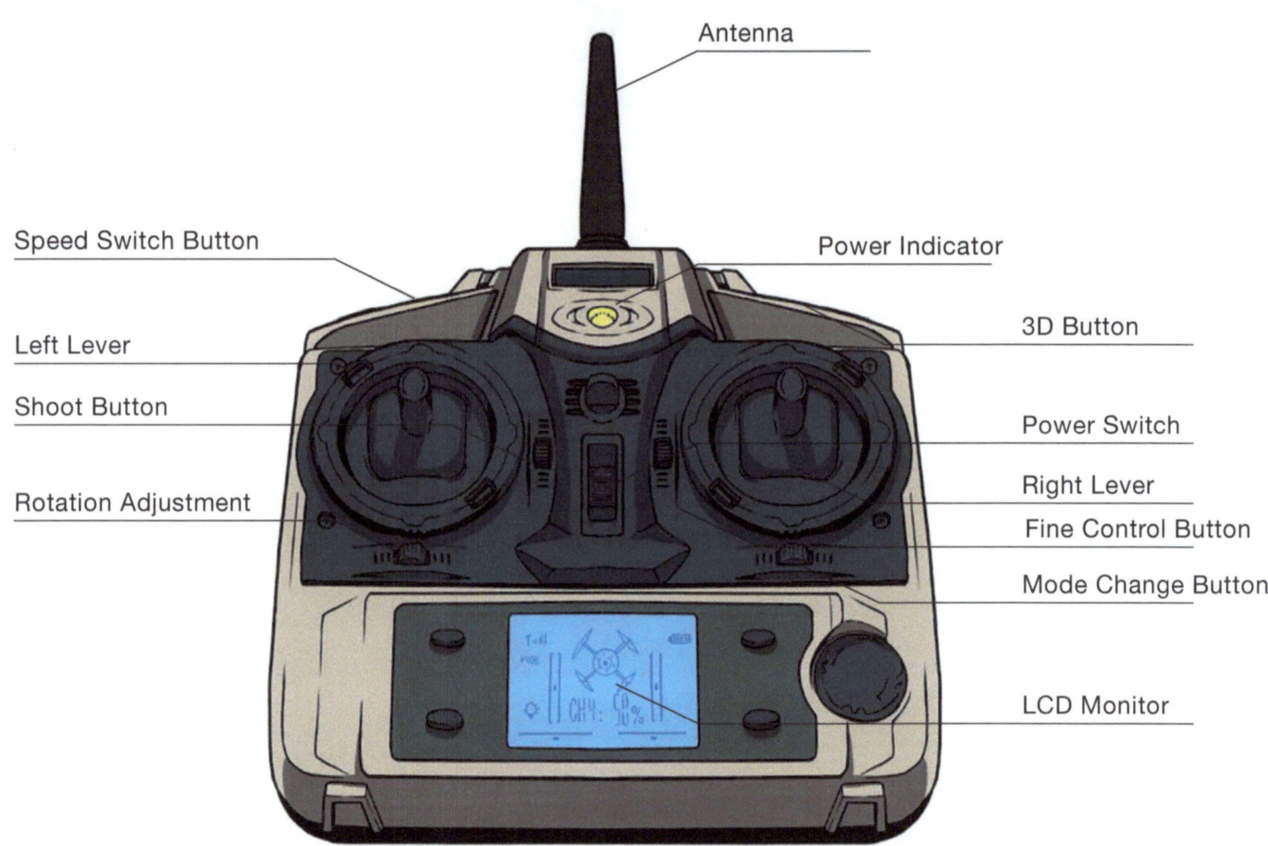

Left Stick	Right Stick
Throttle Rise and lower the height of the drone.	Pitch (Elevator) Move the drone back and forth.
Yaw (Rudder) Rotate the drone left and right.	Roll (Aileron) Move the drone left and right.

The unmanned aerial vehicle, which we often refer to as a drone, refers to a multicopter, a smart flying object composed of several rotating wings, known as propellers. Depending on the number of propellers, they are called:

- Quadcopter (4 Propellers)
- Hexacopter (6 Propellers)
- Octocopter (8 Propellers)
- Multi (Several Propellers)

And so on...
The reason that propellers are composed of even numbers is due to the principle of action and reaction.

Drones can be divided into essential components and optional equipment (including ground support equipment). Essential components are for ground control and mission planning, which control the drones on the ground and analyze the information collected from it. It has takeoff and landing control stations, ground transmissions, reception pieces of equipment, and onboard pieces of equipment. Optional pieces of equipment include ground repeaters, aerial repeaters, launch pads, retrieval nets, remote image reception, detectors, and controllers.

Manned and unmanned aircraft of the same type generally have recognizably similar physical components. The main exceptions are the cockpit and environmental control system or life support systems. Some UAVs carry payloads (such as a camera) that weigh considerably less than an adult human, and as a result, it can be considerably smaller. Though they carry heavy payloads, weaponized military, UAVs are lighter than their manned counterparts with comparable armaments.

Small civilian UAVs have no life-critical systems, and can thus be built out of lighter but less sturdy materials and shapes, and can use less robustly tested electronic control systems. For small UAVs, the quadcopter design has become popular, though this layout is rarely used for manned aircraft. Miniaturization means that less-powerful propulsion technologies can be used that are not feasible for manned aircraft, such as small electric motors and batteries.

Control systems for UAVs are often different than manned crafts. For remote human control, a camera and video link almost always replace the cockpit windows; radio-transmitted digital commands replace physical cockpit controls. Autopilot software is used on both manned and unmanned aircraft, with varying feature sets.

Body or Frame

The primary difference for planes is the absence of the cockpit area and its windows. Tailless quadcopters are a common form factor for rotary wing UAVs while tailed mono-copters and bi-copters are common for manned platforms

Power Supply & Platform

Small UAVs mostly use lithium-polymer batteries (Li-Po), while larger vehicles rely on conventional airplane engines.

Battery elimination circuitry (BEC) is used to centralize power distribution, a microcontroller unit (MCU). Costlier switching BECs diminish heating on the platform.

Computing

UAV computing capability followed the advances of computing technology, beginning with analog controls and evolving into microcontrollers, then system-on-a-chip (SOC) and single-board computers (SBC).

System hardware for small UAVs is often called the Flight Controller (FC), Flight Controller Board (FCB), or Autopilot.

Sensors

Position and movement sensors give information about the aircraft state. Exteroceptive sensors deal with external information like distance measurements, while the proprioceptive ones correlate internal and external states.

Non-cooperative sensors can detect targets autonomously so they are used for separation assurance and collision avoidance.

Degrees of freedom (DOF) refers to both the amount and the quality of sensors onboard: 6 DOF implies 3-axis gyroscopes and accelerometers (a typical inertial measurement unit – IMU), 9 DOF refers to an IMU plus a compass, 10 DOF adds a barometer and 11 DOF usually adds a GPS receiver.

Actuators

UAV actuators include digital electronic speed controllers which control the RPM (rotation per minute) of the motors linked to motors/engines and propellers, servomotors (for planes and helicopters mostly), weapons, payload actuators, LEDs, and speakers.

UAV Software

UAVs are real-time systems that require a rapid response to changing sensor data. Examples include Raspberry Pi, Beagleboards, etc. shielded with NavIO, PXFmini, etc. or designed from scratches such as Nuttx, pre-emptive-RT Linux, Xenomai, Orocos-Robot Operating System or DDS-ROS 2.0.

MJ wants to go back in time.

Minjae is loving drones, he now wants to learn about their origins, and what gave them birth.

02.

History of Drones

Going back in time

It is the main reason that drones were developed for using them at war. Everybody wants to live in peace by making new technology weapons such as Drones, Atomic

Well... that's a dissapointing fact...

Bombs, and other weapons.
Even after making new technology, many people died in the war. Right now, many new technologies are being used for keeping up the peace. Referring to the history of drones, we are using so many new terms for understanding better than ever from now on. Please do not get mixed with all new words and technologies. Multiple terms are used for unmanned aerial vehicles, which generally refer to the same concept.

The term "drone," more widely used by the public, was coined regarding the early remotely-flown target aircraft used for practice firing of battleship's guns, and the term was first used with the 1920's Fairey Queen and 1930's de Havilland Queen Bee target aircraft.

These two were followed in service by the similarly-named Airspeed Queen Wasp and Miles Queen Martinet, before ultimate replacement by the GAF Jindivik.

The term "unmanned aircraft system" (UAS) was adopted by the United States Department of Defense (DoD) and the United States Administration in 2005 according to their Unmanned Aircraft System Roadmap 2005–2030. The International Civil Aviation Organization (ICAO) and the British Civil Aviation Authority adopted this term, and also used it in the European Union's Single-European-Sky (SES) Air-Traffic-Management (ATM) Research (SESAR Joint Undertaking) roadmap for 2020. This term emphasizes the importance of elements other than the aircraft. It includes elements such as ground control stations, data links, and other support equipment. A similar term is an unmanned-aircraft vehicle system (UAVS), remotely piloted aerial vehicle (RPAV), remotely piloted aircraft system (RPAS), and many more other alike terms are in use.

A UAV is defined as a "powered, aerial vehicle that does not carry a human operator, uses aerodynamic forces to provide vehicle lift, can fly autonomously or be piloted remotely, can be expendable or recoverable, and can carry a lethal or nonlethal payload." Therefore, missiles are not considered UAVs because the vehicle itself is a weapon that is not reused, though it is also unmanned and, in some cases, remotely guided.

The relation of UAVs to remote controlled model aircraft is unclear. UAVs may or may not include model aircraft. Some jurisdictions base their definition on size or weight, however, the US Federal Aviation Administration defines any unmanned flying craft as a UAV regardless of size. For recreational uses, a drone is a model aircraft that has first-person video, autonomous capabilities, or both.

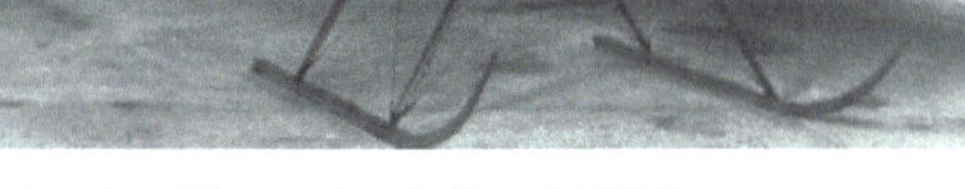

Aerial Target at the WWI

Kettering Bug

Drone walking dog from *Back to the Future*

War, Peace, and Drones

In 1916, during the First World War, the United Kingdom developed a ground - maneuverable military UAV through flight and self - propulsion and the Airy Targets project for the development of defensive flying objects. It was used as a full-width UAV, and also for training purposes. As a result, countries such as the US have felt the need for unmanned aerial vehicles for reconnaissance and combat. In 1917, Peter Cooper and Elmer Sperry of the United States developed an unmanned aircraft called the Spherical Aerial Torpedo. In 1918, Charles Kettering developed a bomber-type unmanned aerial vehicle at GM, one of America's leading automotive companies. When the aircraft reached the target area after the automatic flight, the engine was shut down and the target was destroyed, but the success rate was so low that it could not be used for actual combat.

At the time of World War II, Hitler put the battle drone V-1 into play. The V-1 was able to carry 2,000 pounds of warheads at one time and fly 240 kilometers (150 miles) before the bombing. It was first put into battle with the United Kingdom in 1944 when more than 900 British soldiers were killed by it and about 35,000 were injured. The United States quickly responded to V-1 and Developed PB4Y-1 and

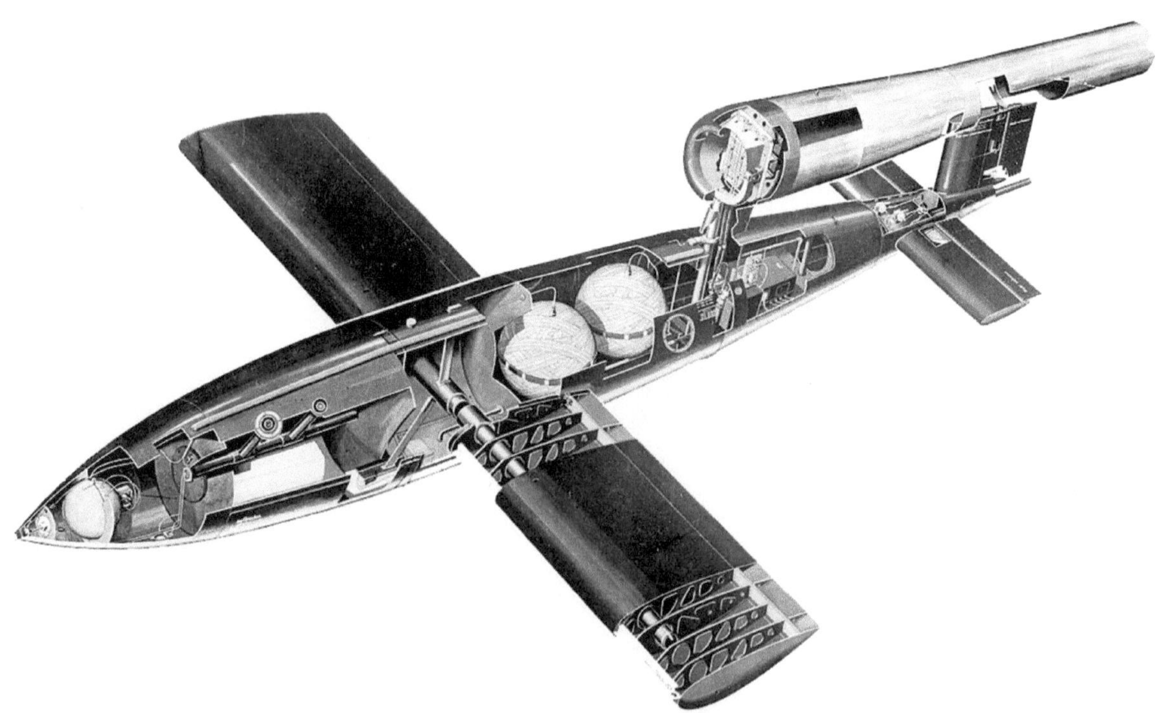

V-1 developed by Germany during WWII

PB4Y-1 of USA

BQ-7. And this aircraft faced the German V-1 route.
In 1978, the Israeli airline developed an unmanned aircraft called Scout, which was put into actual combat in 1982. This unmanned aircraft was equipped with a piston engine, such as an automobile engine, and emitted a small radar signal. Besides, it was impossible to shoot it down. It also enabled real-time monitoring data transmission with a central television camera. In 1982, the aircraft was launched in Israel, Lebanon, and Syria.

It was involved in the Battle of the Valley of the Caucasus, and it lost a battle by destroying 15 of the 17 Syrian missile bases. In 1989, cheap and light unmanned aircraft was created, and Pioneer was able to take off from the ground and ship deck with a rocket engine. The plane flew 533 times in the Gulf War and has been very effective in monitoring and is still in use in Israel, the United States, and so on. In the 1990s, unmanned aircraft development in the United States became active and new models were developed. "Pathfinder" is an ultralight research aircraft devel-

Scout

Pioneer

NASA's Pathfinder, manufactured by AeroVironment, and developed under NASA's Environmental Research Aircraft and Sensor Technology (ERAST) program, was a solar-powered drone/smart flying object (SFO) with the purpose of being used as an atmosphere sattelite.

NASA Pathfinder

oped for environmental research. The aircraft was able to collect wind and weather data through a small sensor.
"Dark Star" was an unmanned reconnaissance aircraft that was expected to have stealth capability of flying at over 45,000 feet, but eventually the development was canceled due to funding problems.

The RQ-1 Predator was developed for pure reconnaissance, and some of them are carrying out successful missions with anti-tank missiles powerful enough to destroy an entire car. The aircraft has been recognized in the Balkans, Afghanistan, and the Middle East. "RQ-4 Global Hawk" is an unmanned aerial vehicle made by Teledyne Ryan, a world-class unmanned aerial vehicle company. The aircraft can be monitored anywhere and monitoring and data transmission are possible up to a radius of 65,000 meters. Finally, the Korea Aerospace Research Institute Developed EVA-3 and successfully tested the stratosphere.

03.

Drone Science

Discovering the science behind
how a drone works

Little Scientist MJ.

Minjae wants to explore more! This time, MJ wants to learn about their science and discover how they fly.

Gravity

Gravity is the pulling force of Earth, and it is understood by Earth according to the principles of Newtonian Incentives. Gravity is the force that the Earth pulls by the laws of gravity.

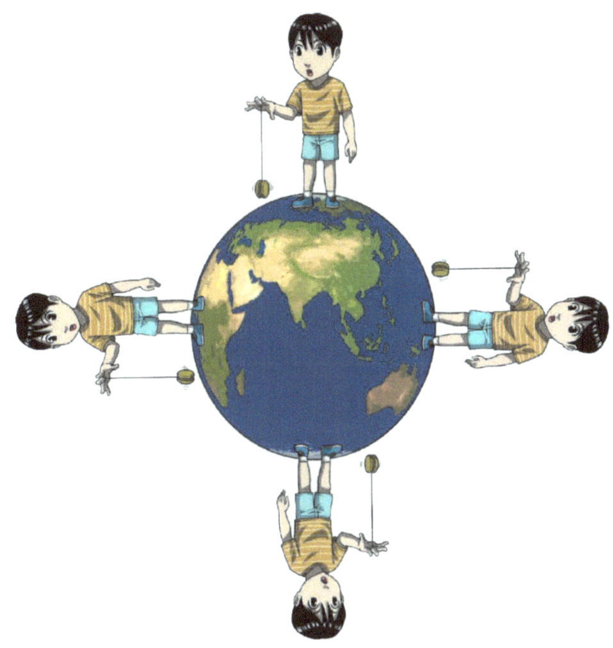

Thrust

The force pushing forward from the rear is called thrust. A typical example is when a rocket flies using thrust or when a propulsion is caused when a balloon has deflated and suddenly flies forward.

Drag

Drag = friction with fluid + pressure exerted by fluid

What do you think drag is?

I know that air is the force that pulls back, but it's not that the air is trapped, so how does it even draw? That's ridiculous.

Exactly! Isn't it ridiculous that air that is not caught is turned off? Can we think about it once?

Have you ever tried walking through a swimming pool filled with water?

Yes! It is pretty difficult to walk through water.

Like passing water through a pool, you get resistance from the water. To pass through a fluid called the air, it receives resistance. And that is called drag.

Lift

Now, let's talk about the most difficult force. It is lift. Two scientists are needed to explain the principles of lift, the first being Daniel Bernoulli and the second being Isaac Newton. Would you like to conduct an experiment?

Go and fetch some toilet paper from the washroom.

Here it is!

Now, fold it in half.

But you said you were going to experiment with the difficult lifting force?

Believe me.

Hold the end of the tissue and blow it over.

The toilet paper flies upwards.

Right, and it shows that the toilet paper is lifted by the wind. Instantly, the pressure at the top of the rest area is low and the pressure at the bottom of the rest area becomes high.

Why are drone's wings even numbered?

The reason that the number of wings on a drone are numbered evenly as 2, 4, 6, 8, and so on is because of Newton's third law.

An example to showcase the principle of action and reaction is that, imagine, Minjae and Aryan are on skates, and are facing each other with their hands on each other's shoulders. When both of them reach out and Minjae pushes Aryan.

Aryan is pushed back, and so is Minjae.

Aryan is pushed back because he has received a force from pushing through Minjae, but why is Minjae pushed back? Minjae is pushed back unilaterally when it acts on Aryan, It is because Newton summarized this as the third law of motion. The forces of action and reaction must be the same and direction is opposite.

Helicopter's tail propeller

A helicopter is of a simple form, rises by rotating the main propeller and the tail propeller which is located in the center of the fuselage, but, could a helicopter fly without a tail propeller?

Consider this scene from a war movie, Black Hawk Down, released in 2001, the scene depicts a helicopter, Black Hawk (UH-60) ignited down very realistically. Black Hawk's tail propeller gets damaged by an enemy shell, rotates around, and crashes against the direction of rotation of the main propeller. The rotational force (reverse torque) is opposite to the direction of rotation of the main propeller.

Because it works on the sieve. This is a scene that shows the principle of action and reaction.

Black Hawk getting shot down from *Black Hawk Down*

Torque

According to the dictionary, torque means "the ability to rotate around a given axis of rotation." However, strictly speaking, torque is not a type of force, but it can be said that it is the efficiency that the force acts on to rotate. Let's simply call it "turning force." The turning force can be said to be a value that not only determines the size, but also the direction in which the rotation is intended.

Torque is one of the most difficult concepts for people learning physics.
For example, consider the event of opening or closing a door. If you try to open the door by pushing the opposite side of the hinged door/the handle, that is close to the rotating shaft, the door won't open well, but if you push the door handle that is far from the axis of rotation, you can open the door well with minimal force.
The force applied to the rotating shaft is different depending on whether the distance from the rotating shaft is close or far. If you consider a seesaw as an example, it will be easier to understand.

Anti Torque

Since most propellers rotate clockwise when viewed from the back, the aircraft tries to rotate counterclockwise, which is the opposite direction, and that is anti torque. Helicopters always need an anti torque rotor to weaken the torque force, and the

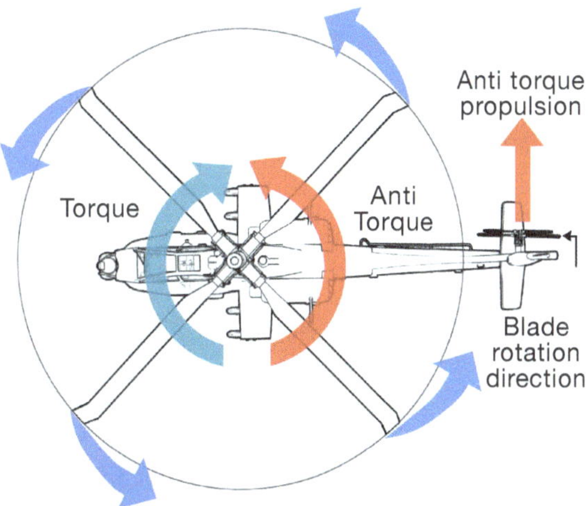

tail rotor does such. The torque of a single propeller plane tends to tilt the aircraft's fuselage to the right or to turn it to the left. Because air resists the rotating propeller, the aircraft rotates in the opposite direction, which is called the reaction torque. This effect is also related to the number of rotations of the propeller, rise or contraction in rotation, and the speed and altitude of the aircraft.

Law of Conservation of Angular Momentum

If no action is exerted on an object from an external torque, the angular momentum of the object is constant.

Angular momentum, in simple terms, is the rotational equivalent of linear momentum and is expressed as

mass × velocity × radius

It is a quantity that must be admitted up to the direction of rotation. Therefore, to remove angular momentum from main wings rotating in objects such as a helicopter, an additional angular momentum must be created. If you don't use additional devices such as a tail wing, the helicopter itself can turn.

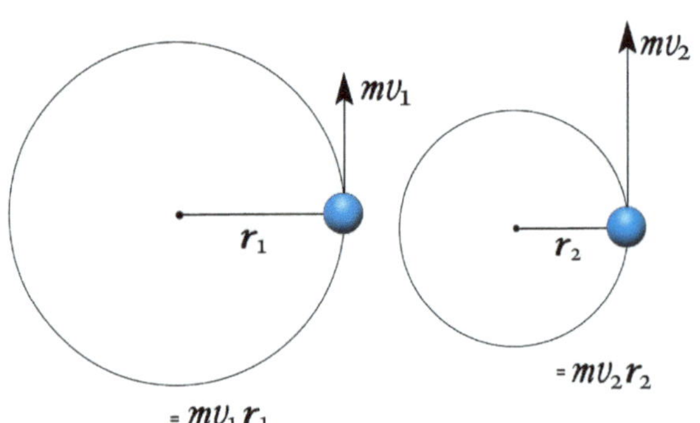

The angular momentum of a rigid object is defined as the product of the moment of inertia and the angular velocity. To eliminate the change in angular momentum caused by torque, the vehicle must rotate in the opposite direction. To prevent an aircraft from rotating, the tail blades must create torque in the opposite direction.

Newton and Bernoulli

When explaining the theory of lift, those who explain lift based on the story of momentum end up with the story of Newton, and those who explain the solar power with force stories end up in the story of Bernoulli as a result and often argue about which theory is correct, but as a result, it can be said that both sides are correct.

The origin of equations for calculating the airflow around an object as we know it including Bernoulli's equation, is merely an explanation by applying Newton's second and third laws to fluids.

You can see books or materials explaining with only one of them, but as we fight with that solely, we come to the absurd conclusion that Bernoulli is wrong or Newton is wrong.

By creating an acceleration, the pressure around the wing changes, and as a result, the speed of the airflow around the wing also changes. The reason why this absurd fight happened is that neither Newton nor Bernoulli ever calculated the lift generated by the modern wing shape, and it was found that people accepted and applied only one of Newton and Bernoulli's theory.

Drone Propellers

Drone propeller blades have different directions of rotation. To be precise, the basic principle is that propellers facing diagonally rotate in the same direction and a different direction from the propeller next to each other. In other words, it is an application of action and reaction, and the anti torque generated by the rotation of two adjacent propellers is canceled so that the fuselage does not rotate and rises upward. Four drone propellers are in one set, and all four propellers rotate in different directions.

Principles of a Multicopter

Before understanding the principle of the multicopter, let's first look at the principle of the helicopter. A helicopter is an aircraft that uses lift and propulsion produced by rotating a rotor. Helicopters fly by creating lift by rotating rotor blades. Helicopters also have four forces acting on an airplane: lift, gravity, thrust, and drag, and lift supports gravity, and if the thrust is greater than drag, it flies in the desired direction.

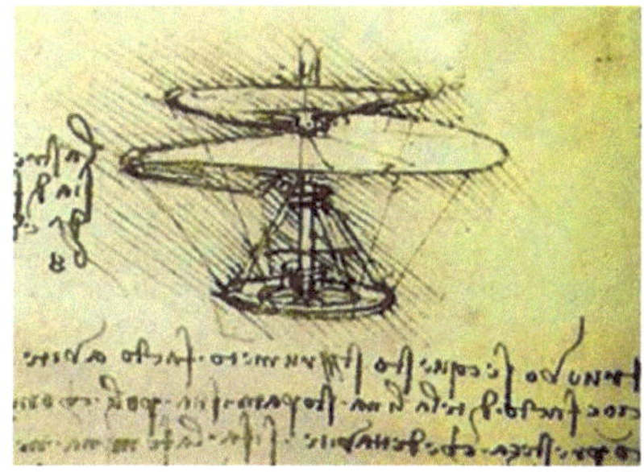

It is hard to believe, but the origin of the helicopter idea can be said to be a Chinese pulley. 15th-century Italian polymath, Leonardo da Vinci sketched a rotating rotor with a spiral rotor.

It wasn't until the 20th century that helicopters that humans could ride and fly were made.
When a helicopter stops flying and remains in its position, this is called hovering. If you think the helicopter is hovering in a windless state, the rotor's rotating surface or the wingtip path is parallel to the horizontal ground. While hovering, lift, thrust, drag, and weight act in the same direction, and the sum of lift and thrust is equal to the sum of weight and drag.

When in the hovering state, thrust is increased so that the sum of lift and thrust is greater than the sum of drag and weight.

When the helicopter starts to fly upward, the sum of lift and thrust is less than the sum of drag and weight, and if we diminish the thrust, the helicopter will fly down.

Helicopters fly forward and backward by tilting the rotating surface of the rotor to the left and right.

Helicopters do not need to run during take-off and landing, and can even hold its position in the air, so they are used for aerial surveying, photography, transportation, fire extinguishing work, spraying pesticides, and also used as military aircraft.

According to the number of rotors (propellers), a multicopter can be divided into a dual copter (2), tricopter (3), quadcopter (4), hexacopter (6), and an octocopter (8)

A helicopter consists of one main propeller, which creates anti torque in addition to lifting, so the fuselage rotates in the opposite direction to the propeller rotation direction.

If you make the tail rotor as big as the main rotor, it becomes a twin-engine. A 'chinook' (dual copter) that can transport many people and tanks. A transport plane is an example.

Multicopters do not have tail rotors. Based on the quadcopter, propellers rotate in the same direction, and adjacent propellers rotate in different directions. Since the two adjacent propellers rotate in different directions, the anti torque is canceled and the body rises without spinning.

Signals recieved from a Drone controller

Drones fly on their own by controlling their flight using a remote controller on the ground or comparing the previously entered GPS flight path with their current flight position (checked through a GPS receiver).

According to the signal used by the controller, it is divided into analog AM (Amplitude Modulation) and FM (Frequency Modulation).

These signals are a purely digital device by coding the modulation frequency itself and has a strong characteristic against miscellaneous waves, but the disadvantage is that the response is a little slow in some cases due to the need for calculation

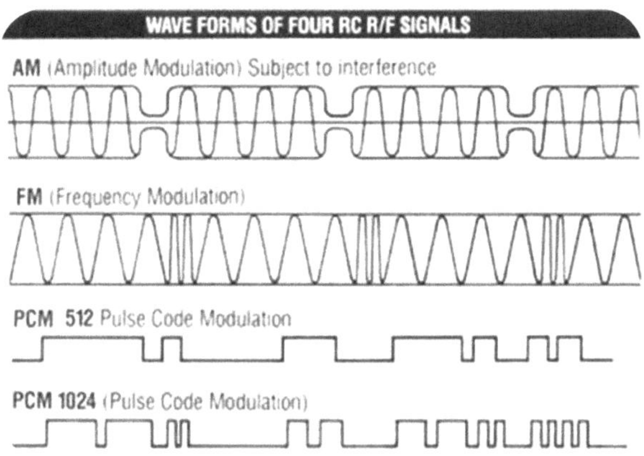

time.
PPM can be described as "mixed positions of multiple pulses." PWM can be understood as "mixing the widths of multiple pulses."

The gray-colored part of the PPM signal is the part that changes when you move the stick of the RC controller to the left or the right.

Recently, almost all regulators use a transmitter that uses a frequency in the 2.4GHz band. 2.4GHz regulators have so many different frequency bands that they rarely overlap each other.

A good receiver has the function of instantaneously converting frequencies and connecting them in both directions to a new frequency band if overlapping frequencies occur.

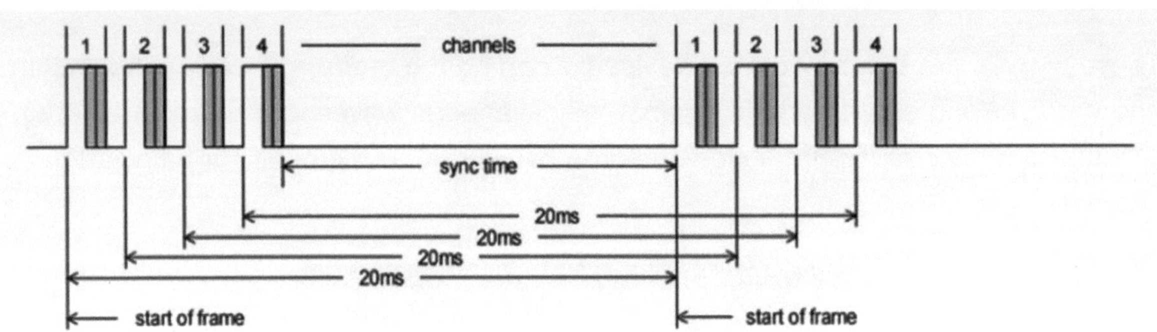

PPM Radio Control Signal

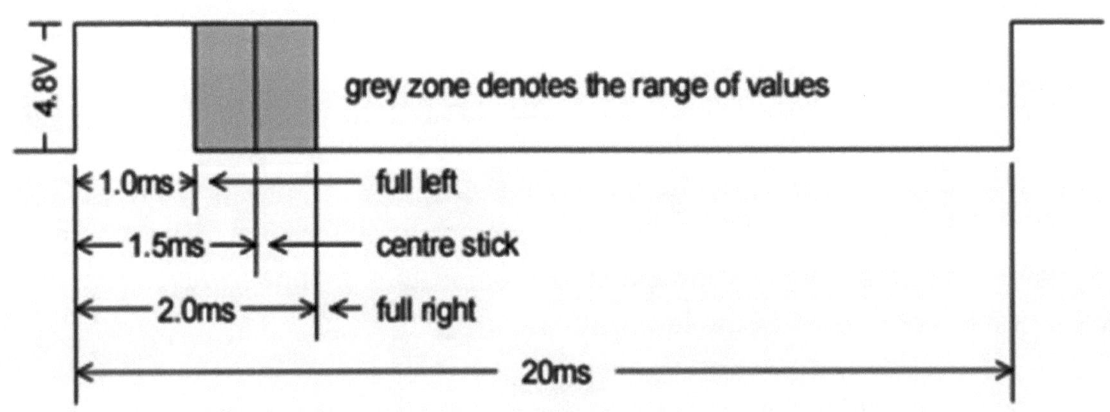

PWM Radio Control Signal

GPS: Global Positioning System

GPS, which stands for "Global Positioning System" is a system owned by the US Government and operated by the US Space Force.

The GPS can find your exact location and coordinates through satellites floating in outer space. The GPS has 30+ satellites orbiting around Earth. As soon as the signals are transmitted to a GPS receiver, 4+ of the 30+ satellites can locate you and calculate your exact coordinates.

Industry Knowledge.

Minjae is even more curious now, he wants to explore the oppurtunities in the industry and how he can be an expert as well, just like his father.

04.

Careers

Emerging oppurtunities in the industry

Developers of unmanned aircraft systems are those who perform the activities necessary to design, manufacture, operate, and maintain unmanned aerial vehicle systems. In addition to developing a sophisticated automated navigation system for unmanned aerial vehicles, it also designs and develops a data acquisition system for UAVs. That's not all. It is also the task of developers of unmanned aerial vehicle systems to build a management system that can analyze and collect systematically the data collected from the air. In the United States, developers of unmanned aircraft systems are members of federal agencies such as the Federal Aviation Administration (FAA), the National Aeronautics and Space Administration (NASA), and the Department of Defense. In recent years, the company is actively entering private companies in preparation for the commercialization of unmanned aerial vehicles.

There is not yet an accurate statistic as to how many people are currently working on the unmanned aerial vehicle industry. However, according to the US Department of Defense, it is known that about 10,000 unmanned aircraft are currently operating, and it is predicted to produce more than $ 89 billion in added value over the next 10 years.

A career is the progress and acts taken by a person during his or her lifetime, in particular those related to his or her occupations. Career also consists of positions kept, titles won, and work done over a long period of time, rather than just a single role.

The drone industry now can develop and create 70,000+ jobs related to the UAVs, including 34,000+ in the manufacturing area and the jobs will also be very high-paying. The U.S. Federal Aviation Administration predicted that there could be more than 30,000 drones in the nation's sky in 2020, also the average annual salary of a drone pilot can be around USD 104,000, and to attain a certificate for being a drone pilot, you will need to have at least 50 hours of training.

Aircraft System Engineer

Nostacotta University in the United States has established a four-year degree program to nurture unmanned aerial pilot and non-inhaled air development specialists in 2010. Recently Kansas State University and the University of Nevada have also set up a degree course in unmanned aerospace research. These universities are also running an intensive training program on UAVs to raise professionals for the vast majority of jobs in the UAV industry. To be a developer of unmanned aerial vehicle systems, you have to complete a four-year regular course in aeronautical engineering, such as sensor equipment, aerospace special machinery, robotics, computer science, etc., and earn a master's degree or higher in related fields.

Unmanned aircraft technology is a new area of fusion technology that requires knowledge and interest in science, physics, and robotics. Therefore, it is necessary to have good communication skills with creative ideas.

Educational Programs

Recently, interest in unmanned aerial vehicle systems and technology is increasing in Korea. In August 2013, the Ministry of Land, Transport, and Maritime announced that it has decided to establish a base for practical application of civilian unmanned aerial vehicles and independently develop civilian unmanned aerial vehicle technology (testing, certification, operational technology, etc.) As a result, I expect that there will be a lot of developers and engineers in the domestic unmanned aerial vehicle system. Unmanned aeronautical engineering departments have also been established in domestic universities such as Hanseo University to provide related education programs. Recently, large companies such as Aeronautics Research Institute, Korea Aerospace Research Institute, Hanwha Corp., and Perstec, and SMEs are actively developing technologies for unmanned aerial vehicles.

Weather Forecasting

Many drones are used for weather monitoring and drone creators like DJI are adding features like GPS geofencing in your drones to keep them out of the areas which are restricted because of the heavy winds, storms or even rain, etc. and they can also result to data such as temperatures, winds, airspeed and altitude using techniques like satellite communications, sensing equipment, GPS geo-fencing or other techniques. One of the companies which very much help in this area is NASA as they made the Ikhana, a remotely controlled aircraft that uses electronic sensor technologies and long-duration Earth observations which also helps in the weather monitoring part. While drones do their weather monitoring job, they also help in disaster management as the techniques used for disaster monitoring are also used for weather forecasting, it's the same, GPS geofencing, satellite communicates, sensing equipment and so on.

Delivery

Drones for shipping packages and all sorts of goods are receiving huge investment from some pretty big players around the globe. With big corporations like Amazon, Walmart, UPS, Google, and other major postal companies investing in drone delivery ventures.

Amazon's program is called Amazon Prime Air, and these drones which deliver are known as Delivery Drones. These delivery drones are used mostly in areas like healthcare and food deliveries. For healthcare, there are always Drone ambulances that come out there to transport drugs and vaccines. For Food, there is the Domicopter which is owned by Domino's to deliver pizzas using drones.

Amazon Prime Air

DHL Drone Delivery

Police

Drones are the latest arsenal for the police, these police drones help in chasing and tracking criminals, tracking dead bodies, detecting if someone is growing any illegal drug at his or her house. Drones lately have been very useful for the police. The first military drone The predator was used to target the terrorist Osama Bin Laden and the first drone killing was done in 2001 when a group of drones shot Muhammed Atel, the former commander for Al Qaeda. The use of drones fitted with digital, zoom, and/or thermal cameras helps law enforcement officers to track crime scenes more reliably and at a safer distance. Quickly deployable camera drone enables officials to have a better vantage point during chaotic situations where the deployment of ground personnel is too risky. Aerial observation points also make it possible for post-accident incidents or crime scenes to be thoroughly recorded and preserved to better explain the sequence of events for each incident. Relying only on ground assets to respond to emergencies increases the threat to the safety of the community and emergency personnel and reduces the efficiency and effectiveness of the emergency response. Drones for public safety function as a force multiplier, costing a fraction of what manned helicopters need. In response to active shootings, IEDs, or armed hostage situations, the SUAS (small unmanned aerial system) can monitor threats from a secure point of view allowing law enforcement to operate more safely on-site.

Agriculture

Agricultural drones are used for farming and they plant crops, flowers, trees, and grains, but other than planting, they also reveal the problems such as fungal infestations, soil variation, irrigation problems, etc. using its bird's eye view, this technique is very useful to the human farmers due to the fact of drone's eyes being much stronger than a normal human's naked eye as the drone can easily detect a fungal or an unhealthy plant and even minor problems. Agricultural drones also help in keeping the record for the crops and maintain data for how the growth of the crop is going, it can detect many small flaws as well. Agricultural drones come very handily to the farmers.

Filming

Drones were introduced into filmmaking as cheaper and safer alternatives for some helicopter shots. They could pull off high-and-wide shots, as long as they weren't too high, sweeping shots, as long as they weren't out of pilot's sight, and not much else, but in the last five years, drone technology has improved, and so has the imagination of the filmmakers who use them. Better camera gimbals, more robust equipment, and more advanced tools have allowed filmmakers to push the boundaries of aerial cinematography. We see cameras flying full-speed to cars and sweeping up seconds before the collision. We 're seeing cameras shoot from the ground and circle around the characters until they reveal the breath-taking scenery. And we see cameras rising above the tree line, only to dip through the treetops to expose a clandestine encounter between characters. The drone is becoming a camera platform on its own — and before long, drones will become part of any filmmaker's tool belt.

Ambulance

Ambulance Drone is a drone designed for emergency medical response and delivery of supplies. Ambulance Drone is a high-speed drone system that delivers AEDs in the event of a cardiac arrest. The drone monitors mobile emergency calls and uses GPS to fly to the emergency site. These drones are capable of saving lives in an emergency. The drone ambulance companies are trying to open lots of centres worldwide so that anybody anywhere can be saved by the drone. The drone will provide the requirements depending on the situation and the problem the patient is suffering from.

Hacking

Not only are drones a potentially catastrophic risk to aircraft, but their radio frequency emissions can interfere with wireless networks and communications systems. With all IT technology, manufacturers and consumers will leave digital doors open. It leaves openings for cyber-criminals and likely cyber-warfares. Drones are fairly inexpensive tools for military use – definitely cheaper than satellite surveillance. Off-the-shelf drones can be used to gather intelligence without any major development effort. The potential for cyber crime – and nowhere are the stakes higher than military drone use. The use of drones must be carefully controlled. The first move is for the government to be fully informed of the risks involved.

Wildfire Mapping

After the use of drones, there was a huge increase in getting lives saved especially in Southern California but before sending drones in the air for wildfire detection, the fire department should have a drone pilot's certification. For the best detection of wildfire mapping, most of the fire departments use infrared cameras that can know the temperature of anything. The future of aerial firefighting will include more drones and self-flying helicopters.

Drone Racing

Drone Racing is a competition that uses FPV drones to race like a car race. It is a futuristic report, featuring an explosive speed sense and a roaring sound like an explosion enough to be called 'F1' spreading from the sky.

GiGA Drones Racing World Champions (hosted by KT) Korea Drone Racing Association Website: http://kdra.org/

Dusie Racing Drones Competition: World Drone Prix 2016 (World Drone Prix)

Other Careers

Drone Design	Drone Designer	Requires Creative Skills
	Artificial Intelligence (AI) Drone	Combination of Drones and Artificial Intelligence

Drone Safety	Drone Engineer	Fix the flaws in a drone
	Drone Insurance Accident Investigator	Insurance policies and collision accidents.
	Drone Security Specialist	Protect your drones and avoid getting hacked.

Drone Racing	Drone Race Track Designer	Design race tracks for drone races.
	Drone Racer	Race drones.

Public Ministry	Drone Police	Search and Arrest.
	Disaster Management	Management and prediction of any disaster using Drones.

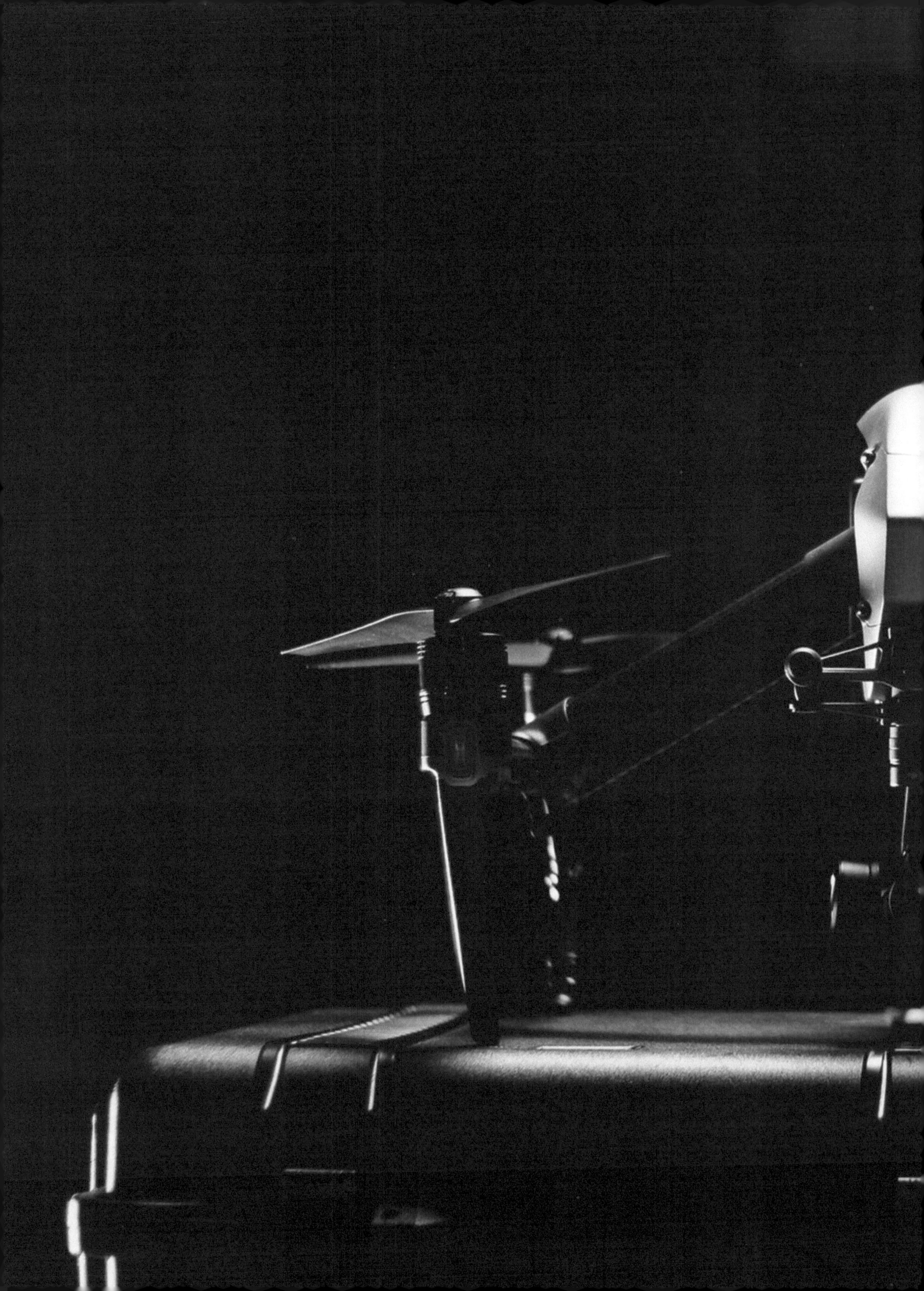

05.

3D Printing

3D Printing

3D printing is the process of generating 3D objects from a 3D Computer-graphics model or Computer-aided design (CAD). 3D printing consists of many methods including depositing, joining, solidifying, and many others. The process of 3D printing is performed by printing many layers of the material.

Usually, 3D printing converged on polymers for composition, due to the ease of production and handling polymeric supplies. Nevertheless, the practice has swiftly developed to not only print various polymers but also metals and ceramics.

3D printing can be highly advantageous for almost everything, including the reduction of manufacturing or production costs. It can produce any type of intricate shapes and designs that cannot be delivered through any other means.

Nowadays, 3D printing is not only being used for manufacturing designs, prototypes, or 3D models, but it is also being utilized for 3D printing food, body organs, weapons, houses, hardware, cars, clothes, furniture, and many other things, including Drones.

The Audi RSQ was made with rapid prototyping industrial KUKA robots.

3D Printed Drones

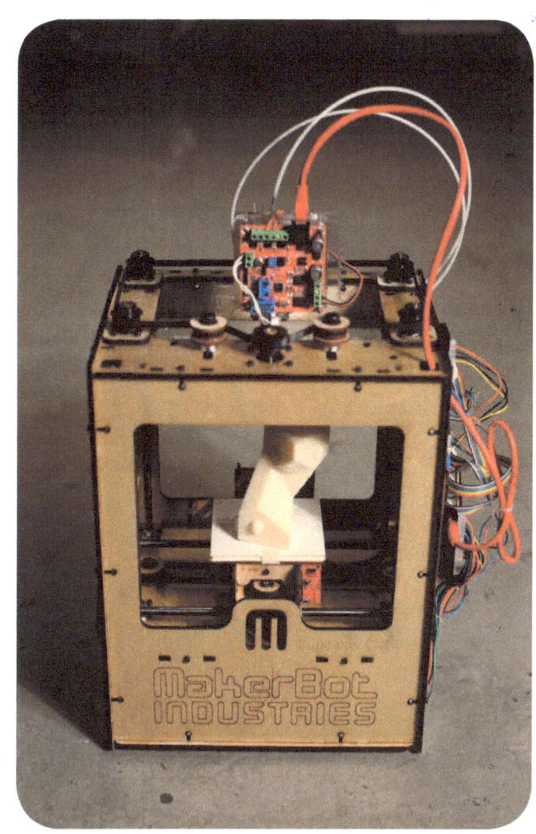

Imagine this, you are a beginner drone pilot, and have never flown a drone before, what are you going to do? You will either learn using a simulator, or by spending tremendous amounts of money in buying a drone you don't know how to fly, and which can lead you to destroy your own drone by crashing it or breaking its parts.

Instead of buying a drone to learn flying drones, the best method is to make your own drone by 3D printing them. If you think you are already too late and have bought a drone, worry not, you can even 3D print your own spare parts if needed in case of destruction of your own drone.

With a 3D printer, you can produce any type of drone you need, no matter how complex its design is, you can also keep upgrading it with no additional costs. If you are not good at 3D modeling, no need to pressure yourself, you can find plenty of free 3D drone models online as well.

Building your own drone out of 3D printed components assists as an exceptional chance to discover how it works and how it responds to the integrations you make.

You can 3D print almost every component of a drone (except the electronic components) including a drone's:

- Propellors
- Body
- Landing gear
- Camera mount
- Prop guards

and many other components...

Even organizations such as Blue Robotics use the 3D printing process for producing their submarine drones.

Other than 3D printing drone components, you can also 3D print its accessories such as:

- A protective case for your drone
- Drone mounts
- Antenna holder
- and much more.

06.

Drone Laws

The Legal side.

There are rules and regulations for everything, just like drones do, and little MJ would like to know about the legal side of drones.

Invasion of Privacy

Drones can be equipped with high-performance cameras, infrared sensors, facial recognition technology, and license plate readers, so you can invade privacy beyond your imagination. If you fly a drone in a residential area, such as an apartment, you can easily shoot the inside of a house.

In Europe, drones were previously used to film the private lives of celebrities, which was very controversial. Recently, drones appeared on the nude beaches of England, UK, and there was a commotion.

Because of the same, the criteria for screening and permitting the flight range and flight conditions of the unmanned aerial vehicle that can minimize infringement of personal information should be established, and it is also necessary to examine and train the institutions or persons that operate and regulate the unmanned aerial vehicle.

Until now, institutional devices have been developed to only limit itself to the distance that the drone can fly and the license for the pilot, focusing on the stability of the drone, but efforts to prevent the problem of privacy invasion that drones can bring are insufficient.

Possible Crimes

Recently, there was an attempt in the UK to smuggle drugs, smartphones, and weapons into a prison using drones. Fortunately, the flying drone failed when it hit the prison wall. Famous singer Enrique Iglesias was injured by a propeller while trying to catch a drone approaching during a performance. In addition, terrorists can deliver dangerous substances in drones, and the danger of being hacked by the drone itself cannot be ignored. In Japan, a small drone containing cesium was found last April in the Prime Minister's residence.

Weaponizing of commercial UAVs

South Korea: South Korea Office of Civil Aviati-on

Under the local law as of 2016, drones are banned from many places in the country, especially from the northern parts of Seoul, where key government offices are clustered. Areas around military installations and nuclear power plants are also no-fly zones. [1] Most of Seoul is designated as prohibited airspace.

South Korea Office of Civil Aviation
www.koca.go.kr

India: Ministry of Civil Aviation

As of 2020, Foreigners are not allowed to fly drones in India. For commercial uses, they need to lend their drone to an Indian passport holder who has the access to gain a Unique Identification Number and an Unmanned Aircraft Operator Permit from the Directorate General of Civil Aviation.

Permission from WPC is required for importing any radio-controlled types of equipment in India, including drones/UAVs. Drones imported into India, without prior permission from WPC and DGCA, will be confiscated by Customs at point of entry. Drones above 2 kg also require a Flight permit and a drone pilot who is least 18 years old and has completed the drone pilot training. [2]

Categories
Drones are classified according to their weight and size, they are categorized as:
- Nano (250g)
- Micro (250g to 2kg)
- Small (2kg to 25kg)
- Medium (25kg to 150kg)
- Large (150kg+)

Registration is required for all listed categories excluding nano.

Required Implementations
- Flight data logging
- RTH (Return to Home) Feature
- GPS (Global Positioning System)
- ID Plate
- Anti-collision Light

Ministry of Civil Aviation
www.civilaviation.gov.in

France: French Civil Aviation Authority

Overflights of nuclear power plants are illegal in France, with a punishment of a year in prison and a fine of €75,000 if an aircraft comes within 5 km horizontally or 1 km vertically of a plant. [3]

French Civil Aviation Authority
www.ecologie.gouv.fr/politiques/drones-aeronefs-telepilotes

Italy: Italian Civil Aviation Authority

Italian Civil Aviation Authority
www.enac.gov.it

Germany: German Federal Aviation Office

German Federal Aviation Office
www.lba.de

References

1. "Regulation of unmanned aerial vehicles: South Korea." Wikipedia. https://en.wikipedia.org/wiki/Regulation_of_unmanned_aerial_vehicles#South_Korea

2. "Regulation of unmanned aerial vehicles: India." Wikipedia. https://en.wikipedia.org/wiki/Regulation_of_unmanned_aerial_vehicles#India

3. "Regulation of unmanned aerial vehicles: France." Wikipedia. https://en.wikipedia.org/wiki/Regulation_of_unmanned_aerial_vehicles#France

07.

Drones on Mars

Multi-Planetary uses of Drones

Terraforming Mars

Earth is currently in a very bad situation, the resources we require for surviving are running out and we, as humans, must take an action towards it. Multi-Planetary terraforming seems like a great idea that can help us replicate all needed resources for survival.

Mars/Space development is very important. Mars terraforming is a "must-do" and not a "fun" to do. Space offers the resources to increase the global standard of living well beyond what it is today, and to do this in an environmentally benign way.

The population of our planet currently stands at 7.5 billion people. By 2050 it is estimated to grow to almost 10 billion. This will continue to compound our drain on natural resources. At the same time, we are stressing the Earth's environment and atmosphere. We are adding millions of tons of carbon and greenhouse gasses to the air that surrounds us and this has already had an impact on global temperatures, which dramatically affects everything. Our planet will reach a point where it will be challenged to support the enormous pressures exerted by a growing population.

Elon Musk, the CEO of SpaceX, wants to build a city of more than 1 million people on Mars by 2050

Elon Musk (left); SpaceX Demo-1 Preflight

Use of Drones on Mars

NASA's Mars Exploration program is all about discovering scientific information and explore Mars to form and early evolve Mars as a planet. NASA has been very active in the exploration of Mars and has been going very prominent so far. NASA has been sending many rovers for the same as well. Recently, in July 2020, NASA launched its "Mars 2020" mission which included sending the Perseverance rover and the Ingenuity helicopter drone to Mars, which is going to land on Mars in February 2021.

The Ingenuity helicopter drone is planned to be used to test the technology to patrol interesting targets on Mars and help plan the best driving course for future Mars rovers. The Ingenuity helicopter drone is the first powered flight on another planet. What is interesting about this helicopter Mars drone is that it requires no drone pilot for it to fly, it can fly itself without any human controls and only minimal instructions.

The Ingenuity helicopter drone is attached to Perseverance rover's belly and will detach once it has landed on Mars.

More information is available on mars.nasa.gov

TOMARS: Multi-Planetary Lifestyle

TOMARS is creating a retail hub to distribute and merchandise space-lifestyle products and services through innovating space-lifestyle by alliances between astropreneurs with space frontiers accelerated through sharing knowledge, experience, infrastructure, and market reach. The startup is looking forward to collaborating with other ventures rather than competing with them. The venture aims to tap into the valuable and unutilized resources of outer space to increase the global standard of living for all and sustainability.

The core founding team is very vibrant which consists of the author of this book, Aryan Tomar, a Canadian who is a tech-genie and the youngest astropreneur in the founding team, Rishkandha – a business of fashion alumni from Polimoda, who is spearheading UX strategy for "Extreme Lifestyle" and has a strong network with luxury fashion industry veterans. Er. Tomar – an XR evangelist who is the Chief Innovation Architect for TOMARS's "Concept Realism Experience Zone." The team brings a strong intellectual network of domain experts from North America, Europe, Southeast Asia, Korea, and India.

TOMARS believes in tapping into the unutilized resources of outer space to increase the global standard of living for all.

More information is available on tomars.space

BTXCity: Voyage for Multi-Planetary Terraforming

Build the Extreme City, or commonly known as BTXCity, is a multi-planetary event and publications brand and is the subsidiary of Pixel Galaxy Studio Pvt. Ltd. BTXCity has a huge history of events organized in the past and has recently announced about their magazine "BTXCity: Voyage for Multi-Planetary Terraforming."

BTXCity has produced various events in the past, and their recent one being the Global Nature Film Festival, which is the first-ever XR integrated film festival. BTXCity also has a very good history with research institutes, ministries, and organizations such as ETRI (Electronic & Telecommunication Research Institute), an AI research institute, NACSI (National Agency of Cognitive Sciences), GL Bajaj Institute of Technology & Management, and many other.

BTXCity declared about their upcoming exclusive magazine focusing on multi-planetary lifestyle, but have not published it yet. The BTXCity Magazine is a magazine like never before, the magazine consists of interesting aviation & aerospace concepts, articles, and stories.

More information is available on btxcity.com

08.

Drone Terminology

Terms frequently used

Binding

After purchase, connecting the controller and the drone one-to-one is called "binding." There are cases where the controller and the drone are connected 1:1, but some controllers can be connected by selecting after saving the connection settings with multiple drones.

The method of binding is different for each manufacturer and model. Most of the binding is done by turning on the drone, turning on the controller, and manipulating the controller controller specifically. If the distance from the drone increases, the connection is disconnected and it cannot be manipulated. Therefore, it must be operated within the distance recommended by the manufacturer.

Frequency

The frequency is the signal section generated by the radio controller to operate the drone. It is easy to understand if you think about the frequency of the radio. A drone that can be operated with a radio controller is classified as 'small power wireless devices' under the domestic radio law. On December 31, 2015, the National Radio Research Institute of the Ministry of Science, ICT, and Future Planning revised the "Technical Standards for Dance Radio Equipment for the Aviation Industry" and allocated a dedicated frequency for drone use. According to this technical standard, the band 5030MHz to 5091MHz (61MHz width) was newly allocated as a drone-only frequency.å

Channel

The channel represents the number of recognizable signals that command the direction in which the drone can move. Drones that require front-to-back, left-right, and up-and-down rotation are mostly divided into 4 channels and 6 channels, and recently, introductory models also support 6 channels. The 4 channels that are used are:

- up and down (throttle)
- left and right (yaw)
- slope (roll)
- forward and backward (pitch)

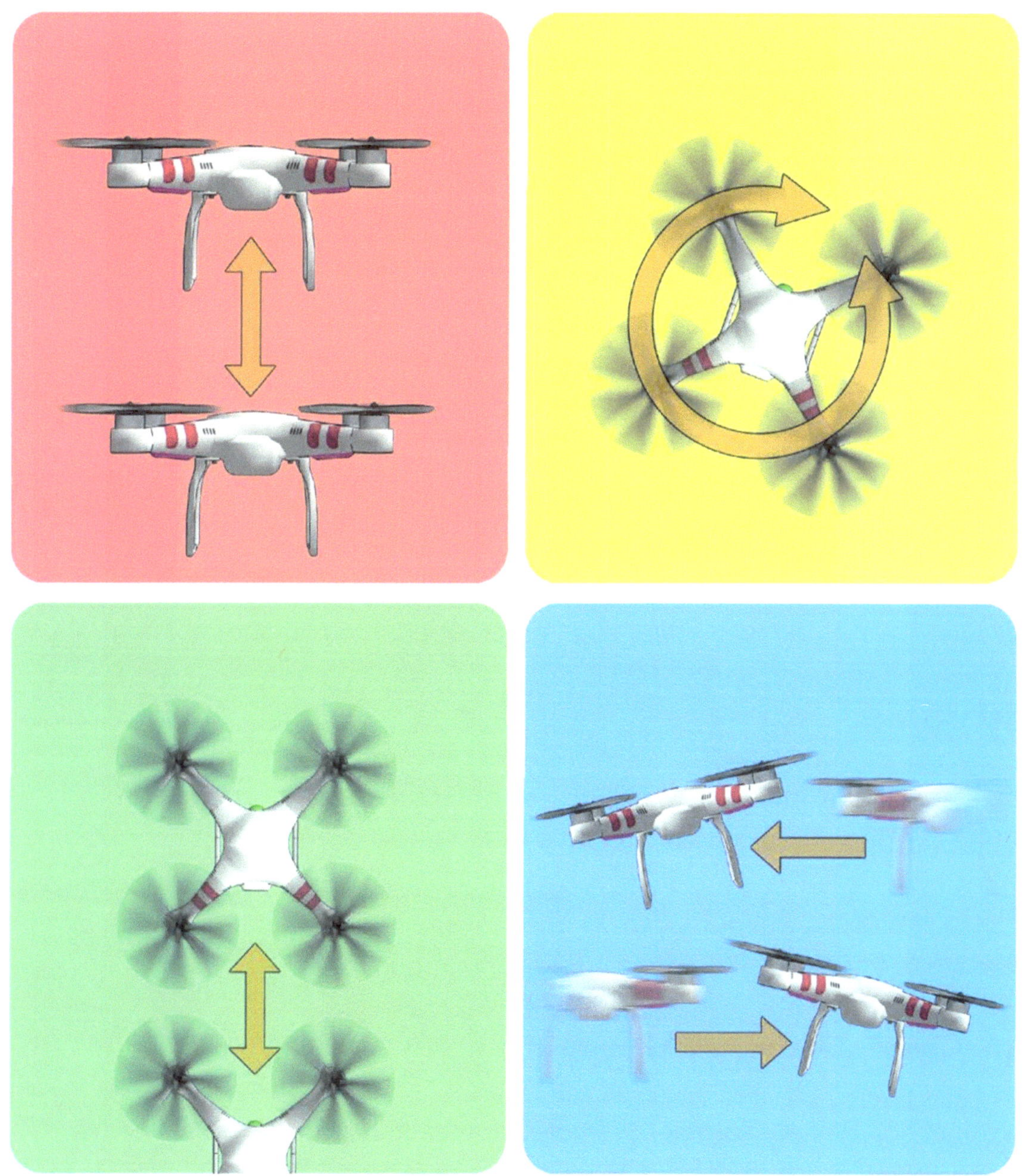

Terrestrial magnetism

Earth's magnetic field is the magnetic field emitted by the Earth. The reason a drone can recognize the direction of travel is due to its built-in sensor that can recognize the Earth's magnetism.

Gyro Sensor

The gyro sensor is a sensor that can measure tilt and acceleration around the ground surface. Through this sensor, the drone can finely adjust the flight by estimating the position of the drone. The gyro sensor determines the current position of the drone and supports tilt. Not only does it not make it possible to make it, but it also maintains the stability level of the aircraft, so it enables stable flight. Gyro sensors are also available in mobile phones, that's how it detects auto-screen-rotations and coordinates the phone orientation accurately according to the phone movement.

Calibration

In most cases, if you fly a certain number of times, an error occurs between the geomagnetic sensor and the wireless controller, so you need to perform calibration periodically. The calibration method is different for each manufacturer and product.

Gimbal

In drones, the gimbal makes it possible to shoot stable and smooth images regardless of the shaking of the camera attached to the body.

In the case of a drone without a gimbal, the movement and vibrations of the aircraft are reflected in the camera to create a trembling image.

FPV: First-Person View

FPV is a function that allows you to remotely transmit video through the camera mounted on the drone and enjoy it as if you are on a drone. It will be easier to understand if you think of first-person shooters such as Counter-Strike, Call of Duty, Halo, Half-Life, and Cyberpunk 2077 among PC games. FPV is largely composed of transmitter, receiver, monitor, and camera.

Hovering

Hovering refers to the state in which a drone is floating and settled in one position. A drone is floating in the sky and will fall if it is not operated. The reason that hovering is the basis of operating an RC helicopter or drone is mostly since it is not properly balanced with radio wave interference.

If a drone moves in a direction different from its given directions and is distorted, the manipulator is confused. In this case, you should always calmly turn off the drone or land the drone at a point where you can see.

If the output is suddenly lowered or raised because the drone is farther away, it is not possible to control it. In cases like these, it is important to stabilize it by moving it little by little.

GPS: Global Positioning System

GPS hovering is a function that automatically hovers through the in-built GPS sensor of the drone. Using this function, the drone can hover to a specific location without calibration or a separate operation. Since the position is stopped at the calculation based on GPS, even beginners can easily hover.

Mode 1/Mode 2

Mode 1 and Mode 2 refer to the type of operation method of the wireless controller and drone.

If you purchase, the wireless remote controller is set to Mode 1 - Mode 4. (Most are Mode 1 and Mode 2.)

In simple terms, it is easy to understand that it is the difference between a right-hand drive car and a left-hand drive car. A right-handle car is a car with a handle on the right, but the UK and Japan use right-handle cars. However, unlike cars, drones have the concept of turning up and down and left and right.

Epilogue

EXT. DRIVEWAY -- LATER

Anderson waves to Lisa. Her big Studebaker drives off down the tree-lined street and away.

Anderson approaches his Chevy. He doesn't take out a key to unlock it. There is no lock. He slides in behind the wheel. Doesn't take out a key for the ignition -- there is no ignition.

A thin METALLIC ARM arches down from the sun visor, scans Anderson's EYES, identifying him. A seat harness wraps around him, and the car STARTS.

Anderson picks up a folder marked "Precrime" and begins to read through the papers. The Chevy backs out of the driveway and takes him to work.

Courtesy: *Minority Report* (Screenplay)

Recalling the scene from Steven Spielberg's 2002 award-winning film *Minority Report* written by Phillip K. Dick, appeared at that time which was a fictitious concept, but now, those floating cars and AI has come to reality where manufacturers from Uber to Porsche, are all now working on flying car and other innovative concepts. Porsche, Boeing, and Aurora Flight Sciences have been working on a luxury flying car concept that will soon be accessible to the public as a transport vehicle.

Why this book?
I am so glad that the young generation of today is so innovative and open to experiment and explore new avenues while they are not exposed to the old traditional "doctor, engineer, or lawyer."

"mera beta engineer banega"
"meri ladki doctor banegi"

The first time I met Dr. Kwon as a special guest at the launch of my first AR book *i Déjà vu* in Tomorrow's India conclave in Shangri-La, Singapore, I discussed with him to compile the content for young generations to make it friendly and entertaining, and soon after, Aryan and Dr. Kwon started planning for a fun version of a drone book.

Dr. Kwon has authored over 2 dozen books while his last 4-5 books were around AI and Drones itself. He has a vast knowledge of AI, Drones, and IP, so it became easy for a Canadian teenager, Aryan to integrate with his **Higher Perspective** of multi-planetary terraforming venture - TOMARS (tomars.space). It was not a surprise when on 25 January 2020, the book was released while my book was released on the same date 25 January a few years back in Singapore.

This book will certainly boost up the youth with an ambitious vision to stand out because you should not be afraid to be different, you should be afraid to be like everyone else.

Drones are helping to ease the consequences of climate change and serve with responsibilities that nature struggles to perform due to the changing climate. I see the passion Dr. Kwon had in delivering the talk at UPES, Dehradun, Uttarakhand, which is known as "Dev Bhumi," on the way back from Dehradun, we discussed how we can deliver a talk for nature relating it to drones, and as a result, we also concluded to be a part of a panel on drones for climate action at the 5th edition of Global Nature Film Festival hosted by BTXCity.

HIGHER PERSPECTIVE

-Aryan Tomar

INT. CIA HEADQUARTERS - PREDATOR BAY - NIGHT

We see a drone-fed overhead IMAGE of the bin Laden house in real time with a resolution of 100 feet. Maya stares at the screen, trying to decipher the shapes moving beneath her, thousands of miles away.

The BLIPS move in increments, shadows lengthen.

Courtesy: *Zero Dark Thirty* (Screenplay)

Kathryn Bigelow's award-winning non-fiction film *Zero Dark Thirty* written by Mark Boal was the perfect example to showcase how Drones are being used by the military, Navy SEALs, and police. CIA's drones did their part for hunting down bin Laden, the armed drones of the CIA flew over Pakistan, but they weren't the ones that killed Osama bin Laden, they assuredly played an essential role in hunting him down.

Although *Zero Dark Thirty* was a nonfiction piece, there are dozens of other fictitious films that revolve around a similar concept, such as *Oblivion* (2013. Joseph Kosinski), *Elysium* (2013. Neill Blomkamp), and *Blade Runner* (1982. Ridley Scott).

Science Fiction isn't fiction anymore.

Space Barons like Jeff Bezos, Richard Branson, Elon Musk, Peter Diamandis, Naveen Jain, and many others are taking leaps to make science fiction a reality.

My interest in aerospace and drones developed way back when I was only in middle school, I loved painting inspired by science fiction artists such as Syd Mead, Chris Foss, Jim Burns, Ralph McQuarrie, and many others. As a matter of fact, those days, I was competing in National Judo competition at Talkatora Stadium, and one of our Judoka unfortunately passed away in a fight, and we had to stop Judo classes and were forced to opt for alternative hobbies and I joined the Aeromodeling club which continue till my college where I took up parasailing at Jakkur Flying Club, Yelahanka, Bengaluru. I have been so passionate about aerospace and aviation, I often take my family to places from flying schools to flying clubs such as Safdarjung flying club and Ambitions flying club.

In my college days, I used to save money to buy myself new games and gadgets, and honestly speaking, Microsoft Flight Simulator was absoulotely one of my favourites.

I even preffered my professional clients who were into the aviation business such as one of my minister client who has his chartered planes and helicopters, he used to fly me for his meetings in his planes and helicpopters, and therefore I couldn't ever negotiate for my consultancy.

There has been a very good response and feedback from the launch for this book in January 2020, but, due to the coronavirus pandemic, there has been complete lockdown globally which feels like a zombie appoclypse, there has been several requests from my EduTech network to package the book as a masterclass for teenagers as the target audience.

I have been the head of IT and Content for Educomp Raffles Higher Education, whereas the parent company ESL was providing education content to over 65,000+ schools, I could see the potential to brighten this generation's youth's future.

We have been very actively conducting workshops in some of the most prominent schools and institutes including GD Goenka, Lancer's, St. Xavier's, PGCIA, GL Bajaj, UPES, and I was amazed to see the vibes and sure enough our upcoming masterclass to be launched at Global Nature Film Festival in association with a Canadian platform which will take this to the global audiences.

Business can be sometimes about being at the right place at the right place and that was the case in December 2018, recently after MJ's birthday, when we visited "Drone Story" cafe in Seoul, we decided to migrate from drone learning to infotainment, and came across Mr. Nick Jo, a man with a very jolly nature, we later signed up with him for his webseries *Aerover* which is a super thrilling award-winning series. We also intend to promote the webseries alongside with *Making Drones with Daddy* (MDWD) to keep learning and keep innovating.

best
of
luck

From Aryan Tomar & Dr. Heechoon Kwon

www.ingramcontent.com/pod-product-compliance
Lightning Source LLC
Chambersburg PA
CBHW050936060326
40689CB00040B/600
* 9 7 8 1 5 4 3 7 0 4 9 6 9 *